GREEN MATTERS™

Making Good Choices About
FAIR TRADE WITHDRAWN

PAULA JOHANSON

rosen publishing's
rosen central®

New York

For our young market gardeners growing up
on Sunnyside and Doublejoy Farms

Published in 2010 by The Rosen Publishing Group, Inc.
29 East 21st Street, New York, NY 10010

First Edition

Library of Congress Cataloging-in-Publication Data

Johanson, Paula.
Making good choices about fair trade / Paula Johanson.—1st ed.
    p. cm.—(Green matters)
Includes bibliographical references and index.
ISBN-13: 978-1-4358-5315-7 (library binding)
ISBN-13: 978-1-4358-5612-7 (pbk)
ISBN-13: 978-1-4358-5613-4 (6 pack)
1. Green marketing. 2. Competition, Unfair. 3. International trade. I. Title.
HF5413.J64 2010
381.3—dc22

2008053527

Manufactured in Malaysia

CONTENTS

INTRODUCTION

Young people who set up a lemonade stand on a summer day both produce and sell a product. They also learn to set a fair price. Many young people work part-time jobs, such as walking dogs, babysitting, or mowing lawns. When a family runs a business or a stall in a farmer's market, the children in that family learn from their parents. There is a lot to learn about the process of buying and selling. The skills learned making and marketing products or selling labor will help these young people make fair deals throughout their working lives. Such skills will even help those teens who plan to earn a living as a professional or executive.

What makes one business deal a fair trade? People have always traded goods, particularly food, clothing, and tools. Trade can be in the form of gifts that people give each other. It can be in the form of bartering, as people exchange one useful item for another, deciding if a bag of grain is somehow worth the same as a chicken—or close enough to be a fair deal. Trade can also go on as commerce between people who don't know each other well or want goods outside of their local area. People sell their work or products for money that can be used later to buy something valuable.

In broad economic terms, a fair trade is a legal exchange of goods and services between buyers and sellers. Fair trade has also referred to U.S. agreements that do not allow a seller to set a price lower than the one given by the manufacturer for brand-name products. But fair trade is more than just making and selling products. It involves fair practices throughout the production and selling of a product.

Most simply, a fair trade is an honest business deal: useful items are exchanged for enough value to sustain the people who made them. It can get tricky when defining the specifics: How useful is an item? How much is an item worth compared to something else? What sustains the people who are doing the work?

Often, these questions are answered with experience. A child who runs a lemonade stand can assess whether or not it's more worthwhile for passers-by to stop by the stand than to take a long walk to a store for a soft drink. After walking dogs for a while, a teen may prefer to learn how to groom them instead to earn more money in less time. Most people believe their work is worth their time when it brings the things that make their lives better. Young workers enjoy earning their own money.

All people want their time and effort to be valued, not just used up or wasted. Anyone wants to trade his or her time and effort for fair value. That is what fair trade is all about—making fair deals locally, nationally, and internationally.

Definitions of Fair Trade

At stores all across the United States, so many goods are sold that it's hard to tell them apart. Labels are used to describe a product, its brand, and other information like its ingredients or production method. There can be words or symbols like "recycled paper" or "shade grown coffee." Many labels allow consumers to make informed decisions.

Some labels can help people make greener, healthier choices. "Recycled" symbols show which paper was made from reused paper instead of newly cut trees. Local food was grown near where it is sold, often within 100 miles (161 kilometers), instead of being shipped to the United States from farms in Chile or New Zealand. The "Certified USDA Organic" label of certain food items means that these items were raised without the use of agricultural chemicals, such as pesticides and growth hormones, and that they meet standards certified by the U.S. Department of Agriculture (USDA). Many people are recognizing newer symbols, such as those for fair trade products.

In Boston, Massachusetts, a participant from Mexico performs a traditional Aztec ceremony at an event where Oxfam America and Transfair USA are promoting fair trade agreements.

FAIR TRADE CHOICES

"Fair trade" is a term that's used by people who want to live in a green economy, where the choices they make about what to eat or use or do will help sustain the environment and communities of people. There are many people who want to use well-made products and eat healthy food. Raising food and making good products is hard work, and such work is worthy of respect. Communities of people who treat each other with respect are good places to live. In a green economy, the natural world is worthy of respect, too.

These Afghan refugees work in illegal carpet factories in Pakistan. Children, some of whom are as young as five years old, frequently work from 4:00 AM to 11:00 PM. They are kept from school, paid little, and often beaten.

Making fair trade choices means being an informed consumer. A person who believes in fair trade wouldn't want to buy a beautiful hand-knotted carpet from Pakistan on sale, or even take it as a gift, if he or she knew it was made by a child who was chained to the loom until that carpet was finished. It's hard to feel well-fed by bananas that came from fields sprayed by planes with weedkiller while the field workers were unable to take shelter. It's also hard to be proud of being the best salesclerk in a store that sells $100 shirts sewn in stuffy warehouses by girls who earned $1 or less per shirt.

If informed, many people would never choose to buy or sell these kinds of goods. It's very upsetting to realize that even if these cruel actions don't happen locally, many products come from places where these actions happen. A fair trade label is used to identify products that are made fairly, without being cruel to the workers.

Fair trade incorporates fair compensation, or pay, for the workers. If you had a job making toys and were paid $1 for each toy, you would be pretty upset if you learned that your boss was selling the toys for $500 each. That wouldn't feel fair. So, even when a company makes a profit from the sale of a product, it doesn't always benefit the worker.

A fancy coffee drink at a U.S. coffee shop may cost almost $5, yet the person who grew and picked the coffee beans may earn only a penny of that price. It is easy to understand that the coffee shop needs to pay its clerks and earn a profit from the sale of the drink. The people who own the company want their investment to make money. The distributor who brings the coffee beans from Central America to the United States deserves a share of the profit, too, as do the truckers who make the delivery. But many people believe that it isn't fair to have all the profits go to the distributor, investor, and retailer instead of the farmer. If the farm worker can't make enough to live on, he or she can't do the work. Without the farmer, there would be no coffee at all!

Fair trade products share the profit fairly. When businesses operate according to fair trade principles, the profit benefits the producer and the worker first, then the retailer. The distributor and the investor

Coffee does grow on trees! Think of how many people are responsible for each cup of coffee, from the bean pickers to the distributors to the person who serves the drink.

get paid also, but they don't take all the profit. If you want to know whether or not a product is fair trade, follow the money.

FAIR BUSINESS STANDARDS

"Fair trade" is a term that was brought to public attention in 1988, with the labeling of several products from developing nations as

TRADE, NOT AID

Many organizations working for international fair trade emphasize the goal of "trade, not aid." They are working together with the United Nations to develop a world trading system that makes it more possible for developing countries to benefit from selling resources and products. Fair trade allows developing countries to prosper and improve their infrastructure, while it makes international aid and money lending less needed.

"fair trade products." From the 1940s to the 1980s, there was an emerging network of nongovernmental organizations (NGOs) working to support fair trade business deals internationally. Usually, these NGOs were private organizations or associations of businesspeople.

Buying fair trade products is a way to show respect for global communities. According to the Web site for the store Green Living, based in Dallas, Texas, "Buying certified fair trade goods ensures an honest and open relationship between producers and consumers across the globe by giving the dignity of fair wages and safe working conditions to workers and high-quality, sustainably produced goods to consumers."

WHAT ISN'T FAIR ABOUT TRADE?

Because people concerned with green living are working now to promote fair trade, it's important to recognize that most international trade is not fair. Most companies from Western nations that buy products from

Industrial disasters harm people and the environment. These people were blinded by poison gas that leaked from a U.S.-owned Union Carbide pesticide factory in Bhopal, India, in 1984.

developing nations do not make the same kind of fair deals with suppliers that they would make with people and companies in their own nations. Often, companies don't pay a foreign supplier as much as they would a supplier from their own country, or they don't pay right away.

Many corporate executives do not take responsibility if their suppliers pollute some distant valley or injure workers. For example, there was an industrial disaster in Bhopal, India, in 1984. Poison gas leaked from a factory owned by an American company, Union Carbide, and an Indian corporation. Thousands of people were killed, and tens of thousands more were injured. Union Carbide paid only a small amount of compensation for a few deaths. Dow Chemical bought the factory afterward but claims no responsibility for compensation. This disaster is one of many that show how corporations of any size, even the largest, do not take responsibility for their actions. Furthermore, many large corporations treat natural resources—such as water, trees, minerals, or crude oil—as if only corporations have the right to use, control, and benefit from them. When citizens insist on honest business methods and responsible environmental practices, they are setting community standards for businesses. Laws exist to support these standards, but they must often be enforced by national governments and by the United Nations. In 1993, Robert F. Kennedy Jr. spoke in Canada at the Clayoquot civil disobedience protest. He said of the peaceful protesters who were blocking a logging road that they were "asserting public ownership over resources which, under Canadian law, are owned by all Canadians, but, in historical practice, were treated as the personal fiefdoms of a few giant timber companies."

WORKING CONDITIONS

In Western nations, community standards for good working conditions are set very high. When a worker puts in an eight-hour shift at a job, he or she expects to receive a living wage, which will be enough for modest housing and food. Workers in U.S. factories also expect to be able to support a family on their wages. Even if they are not members of a union, they expect safe working conditions and that no one will take unfair advantage of them physically, emotionally, or financially. In the United States, workers are protected not only by labor laws but also by community standards.

Workers in many overseas factories receive wages that are much lower than those in the United States. This is partly because the local cost of living is lower, so a smaller amount of money is usually enough for laborers to live on. But what they earn is still not a living wage, as two people or more in a family must work to earn enough for modest housing and food. In those conditions, it is very hard for people to pay for medical care or a marriage or furniture without going into a debt that lasts for years.

Most of the workers who are women or children are paid even less money than men are. This double standard lowers the wages of women and children and devalues their quick hands and stamina. It also treats men as workhorses whose strength can be used up without offending the community standards.

In some countries, such as Pakistan and the Ivory Coast, it has become common for children to do a full day's work, even if they are less than eight years old. Unless these children work, their families cannot afford to feed them, let alone send them to school.

If someone made your little sister or brother work for ten hours every day in a farm or a factory, you would tell the authorities and have them take your sibling to school. If this were the only workplace in town, you could start an alternative business, maybe with help from your family and friends or a small loan from a bank. But most people who work in factories and farms in third world countries don't have the opportunities that you have. Frequently, they can't afford to keep their children in school. Often, the authorities support the only local work available, especially if it brings in money from Western nations. Many times at the end of a working day, people are too tired to start their own small businesses or can't afford to buy tools and materials for them.

FAIR TRADE IN IDEAS AS WELL AS GOODS

There are many ways a person can support fair trade besides starting a business to sell fair trade products. Alan Walker was a graduate

Police raided this embroidery factory in New Delhi, India. Officers and activists of the Bachpan Bachao Andolan (a movement against child labor) rescued thirty-four children who were working there.

student when he first visited Kenya in 1965 and began searching for fossil bones. Settled near the village of Nariokotome, he had just enough money to pay for a cook for his campsite, a goat for his dinners, and a few men to guide him in the dusty hills. Walker couldn't afford a trip to Kenya the next year but scraped together some money a year after that. The villagers were pleased to see him again. His cook was ready, there was a goat for him, and the men had found many fossil bones and would lead him to them. The villagers asked him if he were coming the next year so that they could raise a goat for him. Ashamed, Walker realized he hadn't considered the needs of the village. He was thinking only about the priceless rare fossils.

Kamoya Kimeu's *(right)* open-air fossil studies in Kenya have become legendary. Here, he and another teacher prepare an animal carcass to use the bones for a class in comparative anatomy.

Beginning with modest funding from the National Museum of Kenya and the National Geographic Society, Walker helped organize a simple program of yearly visits. Several men from the area became expert fossil hunters. Together with Walker and the Leakeys, a well-known fossil-hunting family, they found unique fossils. For decades, the "Hominid Gang," as this group of Kenyans is called, has taught the finest field training to visiting scientists from many universities. The Hominid Gang's work not only supports their community and nation, but it has also fostered a center of learning that contributes to scientific knowledge recognized around the world. Their leader, Kamoya Kimeu, became the curator of fossil sites for Kenya's National Museum and is considered the world's most successful hominid fossil hunter.

MYTHS AND FACTS
MYTHS AND FACTS
FACTS
MYTHS AND
MYTHS AND
FACTS
MYTHS AND
FACT.
MYTHS AND
FACTS

MYTH: Profit is always made at someone else's expense.

FACT: All trade is not alike. Honest business offers worthy goods and services at fair value. Dishonest business cheats the customers and the workers.

MYTH: Everybody gets away with whatever they can in business.

FACT: Many business owners choose to meet higher industry and labor standards than those required by law.

MYTH: This product is the "green" version, so everything's done right to make it.

FACT: Read labels carefully, and do research. Just because something is labeled "green" or even "certified organic" doesn't mean the workers who made the product are paid a living wage to do work that sustains the environment.

CHAPTER ②

Production of Fair Trade Goods

Fair trade goods and services are produced in working conditions acceptable to union standards or Western labor standards. Although this makes a big difference for factory workers in developing nations, it makes even more of a difference for farm workers.

Work on a farm has always been hard during planting and harvest seasons. Modern factory-farming methods don't change that. Modern farming just uses tractors and tools to spread that hard work over a wider area of cleared land.

Traditional farming methods varied from country to country. Often, small fields were planted with a variety of seeds saved from the previous year. But with colonialism, many traditional farming methods were lost. Modern farming methods seemed productive as long as there was fuel for the tractors and fertilizer to spread. But this fuel and fertilizer are made from petroleum. They are expensive. Most farmers who used to work a few acres could not

Anywhere in the world, produce that is sold with a fair trade label has been raised and harvested by workers in good conditions who are paid a fair share of the selling price.

afford to buy large fields and tractors, not to mention fuel, fertilizer, and seeds. So, many small farmers became farm workers, often working on large properties owned by foreign investors. Most modern farming methods are sustained by the hard work of people who do not get the full benefit of their work. With their hard work and low wages, farm workers in third world countries are supporting affordable food and cotton clothing for people in Western nations.

Since about 1980, there have been more opportunities for small farmers to relearn traditional farming methods. The result has been increased production and opportunities to market their produce. When small farmers can sell some of their produce to a regional or

ONE COMPANY'S INFLUENCE

It's hard to calculate the influence of a single company on a nation's economy. In his book *Fast Food Nation*, Eric Schlosser wrote that food-service retailer McDonald's is the largest purchaser of beef, pork, and potatoes and the second-largest purchaser of chicken in the United States. This buying power gives the company an unprecedented degree of influence over the nation's food supply. McDonald's has employed an estimated one in eight American workers. Labor laws and business regulations that affect this company will have a major impact on the fast-food industry and the national economy. The business standards of a company this size (with more than thirty thousand restaurants worldwide, according to http://www.mcdonalds.com) will influence other corporations around the world.

international buyer, the income can make entire communities prosper. With support from their buyers, small farmers can form collectives and certify their produce as organic. Organically raised produce usually sells for a higher price. Though all certified organic products are not fair trade products, most fair trade products meet the standards for organic certification. Most are also environmentally sustainable.

There is plenty to learn about the farm workers who grow the food that you buy from overseas. Read the labels and pamphlets that are provided with these various products. Go to company Web sites to learn more about the products around you. It may be upsetting for you to learn how hard life is for the people who make the goods and products that you use every day. Some of your choices can support a better life for the people around you, for fellow citizens across your nation, and for people around the world.

WHERE ONE PRODUCT TAKES US

It's easy to think a bicycle would be a "green" choice for travel because it doesn't require gasoline and, thus, doesn't pollute the environment. But is it a fair trade product? Riding a bike is exercise, which promotes good health. Bikes are much cheaper to buy than cars and involve fewer ongoing expenses than daily bus fares. A little maintenance should keep a bike rolling for years. But there are questions to ask about bicycles, and the answers may be surprising. Not all of them are equally "green." In particular, not all bikes are fair trade products. Looking at three different bikes, for example, will let you compare them to see how well they can be defined as fair trade products.

There are many affordable bicycles available at department stores and sporting-good stores that go for $100 to $200. A low-cost bike sold in a national chain that maintains a good working environment for its clerks sounds as though it would be a reasonable product to buy. But if that bike is ridden to class by a student every day or to work by an adult every morning, then it will wear out in less than a year. That bike is affordable because low-wage workers made the frame in China. The pipes are heavy and brittle, and the joints are made by lower-temperature brazing instead of welding. A child would be able to ride such a bike for a year or two before growing out of it. The weight of an older teen or adult is enough to stress the frame so that the joints fail. This may be an affordable bike, but it's not a fair trade product. The workers are paid less than industry standard and produce low-quality products in bad conditions.

Another choice for cycling could be a recumbent tricycle. There are several models designed for speed or stability and built by small companies in North America, Europe, and Australia. Because only a few hundred tricycles of any one model are made, a recumbent tricycle

A farmer and two of her children are working the family's field in Uganda. As local chair of her community development program, this farmer learned to increase the quality and production of her crops.

is sold for $1,000 to $7,000. The price of the product is directly related to the cost of production. An ordinary bicycle for similar purposes, from recreation to racing, would cost only $300 to $3,000 because unskilled workers make thousands of them. Instead of being mass-produced by a series of workers in a large factory overseas, the recumbent tricycle has been hand-welded by a well-paid worker in a small factory. The worker sees each trike through the process from start to finish, just like the highest-quality custom-made projects. Buying one of these recumbent tricycles supports a small independent company, usually a

A health-care worker in rural Bizana, South Africa, uses a Kona AfricaBike to visit a patient. AfricaBikes have enabled health-care workers to deliver medicine to many patients in a day instead of walking rough roads to only two or three homes.

family-run business with fewer than a dozen employees. The company may also support strong programs for recycling and community development. A recumbent trike may not be as affordable as an ordinary bicycle. But it is a quality product that is fairly traded from one part of the United States to another, or from one developed nation to another.

A third bicycle to consider is the AfricaBike, made by Kona for the BikeTown program. The donation of thousands of plain, strong bikes to nurses who deliver AIDS medications has benefited communities in Botswana, Mozambique, Swaziland, and South Africa. Parts for these bikes are made in many countries worldwide. The frames are made at an assembly plant in Taiwan; Kona inspects the plant monthly. The single-speed bikes with coaster brakes have no cables or brake pads to fray and wear out. The frames can be repaired by welding, unlike the lighter alloys that are used in many modern bikes.

There are no bicycle makers in these African countries, so shipping in bikes does not take away from local business. In fact, the AfricaBike program trains local handymen, giving them tools and materials to make repairs for these and other bicycles. The AfricaBike is a reliable product built for an American/Canadian-owned business that supports community development programs in Taiwan, the United States, Canada, and several African countries. It creates opportunities for small business development. It's an example of how fair trade goes in all directions.

CHAPTER 3

Lasting Effects of Fair Trade

Fair trade is more than just a good idea. There are reasons to promote fair trade, which will benefit small businesses and large corporations. People make business decisions not only to be honest and fair but also to earn a profit. A business that relies on fair trade may not make profits quite as big as those of a company serving only its own interests. But a fair trade business will earn reliable profits over a longer period of time and will benefit from a stronger economy.

FAIR TRADE OR FREE TRADE?

Free trade agreements between countries often give investors opportunities to profit from using up resources and workers in other nations. These agreements can also result in funneling natural resources into short-term development projects, such as a cobalt mine or the clear-cut logging of tropical mahogany trees. The investors are

These children in Bolivia now have a school, which was built with a share of the profits from the fair trade coffee collective in their community. Roads and other public works systems benefit, too.

not responsible for the local ecology, pollution, or workers, and laws are often not enforced. Investors may not be concerned with a foreign nation's long-term economic future, only their own short-term profit. Free trade agreements allow corporations the freedom to use up natural resources in less developed nations. It is important for these trade agreements to be written carefully in order to encourage those investors who support the sustainable development of resources.

Trade agreements can promote fair trade. The goal is to use natural resources in ways that can be sustained for local and regional benefits. With fair trade, a developing nation can afford to build not only factories but also schools and hospitals. Workers employed under fair trade principles tend to be healthier and better educated, and do better work than those who aren't. For example, there are several companies that run telephone service centers throughout the world. Some companies have centers in countries that have strong labor laws for good working conditions. Employees at these centers are literate, and rarely absent from work, and make few errors. By contrast, service centers in countries without strong labor laws are often unreliable.

Investors from Western nations are just as free to invest in countries with agreements that promote fair trade. They may earn a more modest share of the profit, but that share will last much longer. The profits will also be more reliable because the local economy will be supported. Trade agreements can support fair trade so that many people benefit, instead of drawing off profit overseas while leaving behind pollution and work-related illness as a local concern.

JUSTICE AND ECOLOGY

The primary goal of fair trade is to treat people fairly. Justice is not solely for criminal courts. Many international groups, such as Global Exchange, work for social and economic justice. These international organizations consist of private individuals, businesses, and some government agencies working together. One of their goals is to shift the focus of the world's economy from currency to community. For example, Global Exchange is trying to transform the global economy from being centered on profit to being centered on people. Many organizations work for international fair trade instead of a globalization that values technology at the expense of workers and the environment. These organizations work to ensure that human rights are protected in all countries. They also promote the sustainable use of technology in local and green economic development.

THE BALL'S IN YOUR COURT

Not many sports fans know where sports balls are made. Three-quarters of all the sports balls in the world, including soccer balls, volleyballs, handballs, basketballs, and medicine balls, are made in factories in Sialkot, Pakistan. Many of the workers in these factories are underpaid, even by local standards. Children are the preferred workers in many Sialkot factories because they are paid less than adults and are more easily controlled by their bosses.

NOTHING IS BEING SAVED

When Americans buy goods at discount stores, they may pay less for products. But the prices are less because the discount stores usually are not paying for business expenses, such as employee health care. Customers may care only about the low price, but this low price comes with other costs. Many products are made in China or other overseas countries by workers who put in long hours for low pay. These products sell in the United States for less than a similar product made locally. Their popularity may suggest that people value a low price more than fair working conditions or domestic goods.

But Americans are learning they don't save any money by buying products made overseas in factories with bad labor standards. They are buying inexpensive products made with cheap and often exploited labor. They may also be buying international resentment, which can contribute to conflicts and unstable international stock markets.

These protesters object to sweatshop working conditions. People can learn where and how their clothes and shoes are made. Labor laws mean that corporations must be held responsible for low pay or unhealthy working conditions in factories.

The word "slave" is sometimes used to describe workers who make these cheap products. United Nations (UN) spokespeople and delegates used the word at the 2008 Global Initiative to Fight Human Trafficking (GIFT). The UN considers thousands of workers in Asia and Africa to be victims of slavery. These workers are tricked or stolen, often across national borders. They are forced to work in dangerous conditions. They cannot leave. They suffer. They are bought and sold on the installment plan by companies and customers who buy their products and don't share the benefit fairly.

It's hard to blame any particular company or product for these unfair actions. Many corporations are responsible, and by association, customers are, too. There is one example that stands out among many similar incidents. Nike paid basketball star Michael Jordan more to endorse the Air Jordan shoe than it paid all thirty thousand of its overseas workers who made the shoes. In August 1992, Jeffrey Ballinger wrote an article for *Harper's* magazine about the pay that Sadisah, a worker in an Indonesian factory, received that April. The factory was a subcontractor for Nike. Sadisah was paid 14 cents an hour for assembling thirteen or fourteen pairs of shoes a day. Ballinger observed that "in order for Sadisah to earn as much as the $20 million annual endorsement fee paid by Nike to basketball superstar Michael Jordan, she would have to continue working six days a week, ten and a half hours per day, for 44,492 years."

It'll take a lot of effort by many companies to make up for such business decisions. Nike and other corporations are working to improve wages and conditions for their workers. Despite this, in August 2008, Australian reporter Mike Duffy exposed bad working conditions, as well as withheld wages and passports for foreign workers, in a factory in Malaysia that makes shoes for Nike. "The real way to address this is for the brands to collaborate and agree on a core set of standards," said Erin Dobson, Nike's director of corporate responsibility communications, in a quote from the *Oregonian* newspaper.

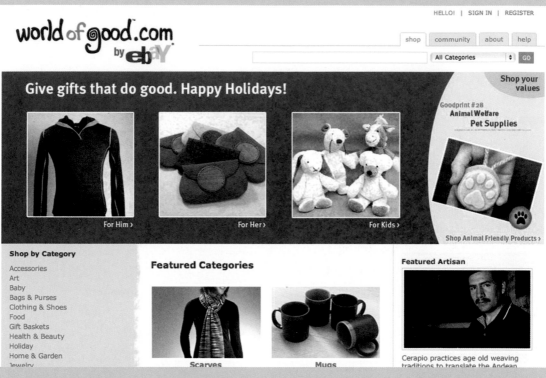

Many stores and Internet businesses, such as World of Good by eBay (http://worldofgood.ebay.com), work hard to use fair trade principles when buying and selling goods that are made around the world and sold internationally.

ONE PURCHASE AT A TIME

There are a lot of products for sale all over the United States. It can be very confusing to think that some of these products are fair trade while others are not. Customers can't always visit every work site to see for themselves how products are made.

Online shopping provides an international marketplace. Not all products sold online are green or fair trade. A group of organizations called Trust Providers has teamed up with eBay to form a new fair trade organization called World of Good by eBay. Participants in World of Good must verify that their companies follow fair trade principles. Their business ethics must empower the workers, artists, and farmers who produce their products at competitive prices.

Some people give up on trying to find fair trade products, saying to themselves, "It's only one purchase. One purchase does not make a difference." But the fact is, one purchase really can make a difference.

One purchase can support a person for an entire year, as many farmers sell their year's crop to one corporate buyer. One purchase by a corporate buyer can support a factory for a year. A factory is often a town's primary industry and major employer. One purchase can also be one of thousands of identical purchases of consumable goods, as most students and workers in Western nations start their day with coffee, tea, or cola. One purchase of a single item, such as a fair trade chocolate bar or a fair trade soccer ball, can encourage a person to change his or her buying patterns permanently. An entire community or industry can be affected because of the actions of just a few people.

ONE PERSON CAN MAKE A DIFFERENCE

Jacob Levitt learned about child labor for a school assignment in sixth grade in 2008. It particularly upset him to find out that oppressed children make most soccer balls. When he began middle school, Levitt took on a social justice project as part of the preparation for his bar mitzvah. Combining his love of sports with his feelings of injustice over child labor, he convinced the Northampton Soccer Club to begin using fair trade soccer balls from Fair Trade Sports. His ongoing plans include encouraging the Northampton High School and the Recreation Department for the city of Northampton in Massachusetts to team up with the Soccer Club for affordable bulk purchasing of soccer balls.

Another person who made a difference is Craig Kielburger. He was twelve years old when he founded Free the Children in April 1995 with eleven school friends. He read in a local newspaper about Iqbal Masih, a boy in Pakistan who was sold into slavery. For twelve hours each day, six days every week, Masih was made to work tying tiny knots in handmade carpets for export. He escaped captivity and rejoined the members of his family, who had been tricked by his captors. He spoke out in public about slavery and children's rights before being shot and killed to silence him. This incident was the first that Craig Kielburger ever knew about child labor, and he set out to do what he could to help stop it. A year later, on a fact-finding mission in south Asia, he began to focus the attention of the international press on the worldwide epidemic of child labor abuses.

Free the Children has become an internationally registered charity. It is the world's largest network of children helping children through education and development programs in forty-five countries. The charity has built more than five hundred schools around the world, and more than one million young people have been involved. The organization has formed partnerships with school boards and Oprah's Angel Network, which is a public charity founded by TV talk-show host Oprah Winfrey. Free the Children has received the Human Rights Award from the World Association of Non-Governmental Organizations and the World's Children's Prize for the Rights of the Child.

WORKERS AND ENVIRONMENTALISTS

The fair trade movement is concerned with the environment as well as with workers. Some businesses offer a matching donations program for employees. For example, when an employee of Disney Interactive Games makes a tax-deductible donation to a registered nonprofit society, the company matches that amount of money. Other companies offer a volunteer program for employees as a benefit. Employees of The Body Shop can commit to a number of hours of volunteer work for a registered nonprofit society of their choice each year, and they will receive their regular wages from The Body Shop for this charity work. Many companies offer incentives like these.

In 1995, at age twelve, Craig Kielburger and his friends convinced the mayor of Toronto, Ontario, to ban fireworks made by child laborers and testified before the U.S. Congress about child workers.

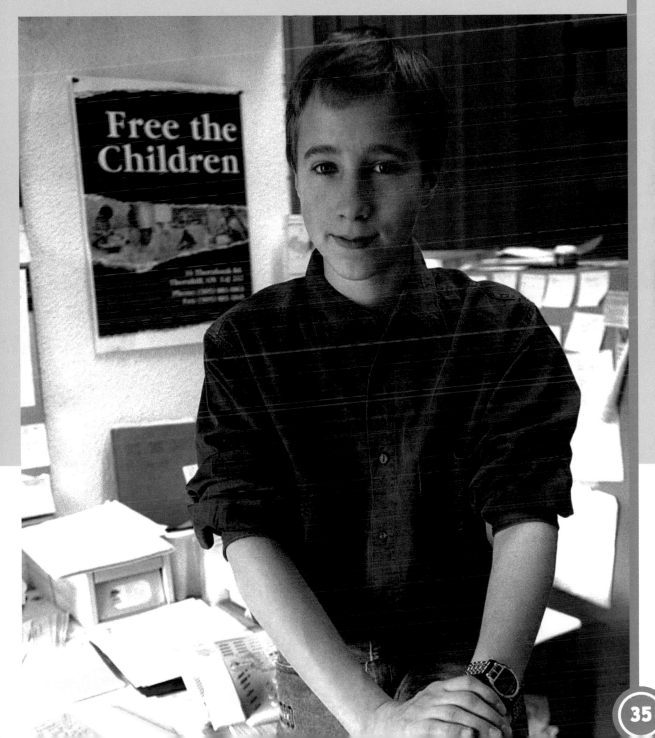

Unfair business practices use up and ruin resources and cause pollution in the United States and in other countries around the world. Large corporations often resist anyone's efforts to hold them accountable for the use of natural resources. Some corporations use their employees as resources that can be used up and forgotten about when there is no more coal to dig or trees to cut. Only the most responsible companies take care of workers who are injured or made sick by pollution. Laws are not enough to make a corporation use sustainable methods—unless those laws are enforced. Public protests can bring local concerns to a national or international audience.

Many businesses, including The Body Shop, are run by people who are proud to support workers' rights and promote sustainable development. Find out where products come from and where the company's money goes.

Corporations often claim that people who protest a company's environmental policies are professional activists, not local workers. These claims don't have to confuse the public. Look to newspapers and reports on radio and television for interviews with local residents. If there are statements from activists, find out about the activists and their motivations. Some are spokespeople for respected groups that work with citizens and governments to promote sustainable resource use. Look in locally produced magazines, as well as Web sites and newspapers. It's common to see local writers present their opinions against "multinationals [multinational corporations], whose business practices often default to sucking resources dry and exporting profits away from local communities," as Geoff Olson wrote in *Common Ground* magazine.

Sometimes, statements from the trials of people charged during public protests are reported in newspapers. In a classic example, Merv Wilkinson was among the Canadian protestors arrested in 1993 at Clayoquot for putting up a roadblock to protect an old-growth forest. At the trial, Wilkinson said, "I am the operator of a forestry [business] that has harvested timber for 45 years off the same land and still has the forest. Now, at 80, I simply must defend what is left of my country from the multinationals of vandalism." The roadblock and campaigns against buying products made from old-growth wood had some effects on industrial logging practices in Canada. In 2000, the Clayoquot area was named a United Nations biosphere reserve, but the reserve did not give legal protection to the Clayoquot area. In 2008, clear-cut logging began in the reserve.

TEN GREAT QUESTIONS TO ASK A
COMPANY EMPLOYEE ABOUT A PRODUCT

 1. Who makes this product, and where do they live?

 2. Do you personally use any company products when you're not at work?

 3. What portion of the retail price for this product covers material production costs?

 4. What can you tell me, in person or on your company's Web site, about this product's environmental and economic footprint?

 5. How does this product compare to other domestic and foreign products?

 6. Is this food organically raised, and were the farm workers the owners, locals, or migrant workers?

 7. Were the workers who raised this food, worked these resources, or made these products protected from exposure to industrial pollutants and chemicals like agricultural pesticides, petrochemicals and hydrocarbons, and toxic materials?

 8. Does your company have a profit-sharing program, and are details available on its Web site?

 9. What community development programs does your company maintain?

10. Does your company pay overseas workers and suppliers according to the terms acceptable to your U.S. standards (contracted prices, prompt payment, accurate product weighing/count, and safe and sustainable working conditions)?

Making Fair Trade Choices

It's not hard to begin making a few choices to increase your use of fair trade goods and services. Start with the three C's of easily available fair trade products: coffee, chocolate, and clothes. These products are available at stores throughout most U.S. cities. They are also available online and by mail-order delivery to anywhere in the world. When you use any of these products, you can make a choice to support good business practices and good working conditions. These are entry-level fair trade products, for beginners.

COFFEE

Coffee is made from roasted beans or the seeds that are inside berries of bushes called *Coffea robusta* or *Coffea arabica*. The bushes were native to Arabia but are now grown in many countries in Africa and Central and South America. It may be a luxury item, but coffee seems essential

When fair trade coffee beans are bought and sold around the world, a fair share of the money earned goes to the people who work for fair trade coffee plantations.

to many people. In Western nations, many people start their day with a cup or two of the dark brew, whether at home or at a coffee shop.

One cup of coffee may taste different from another, but there is a far bigger difference than taste between an ordinary cup of inexpensive coffee and fair trade coffee. Most of the cheap coffee that is sold in grocery stores or served in restaurants is made from high-caffeine robusta beans. These beans are roasted and ground in huge batches and eventually go stale in their packaging for supermarkets or restaurants. It's worth paying a little more to get arabica beans. These beans have more flavor oils and less caffeine. They taste even better when roasted in small batches and freshly ground.

Coffee bean production is of higher quality on small organic method farms. There, the bushes are shaded by biologically diverse trees that provide traditional nuts, fruits, and lumber to the farmers. There is no need to clear and plow hundreds of acres for planting, or to spray weed- and bugkiller. Good working conditions for farmers are good for growing better beans.

Unfortunately, the majority of coffee sold worldwide is made from robusta beans that are grown on larger plantations using agricultural chemicals. Small farmers are under pressure to accept low prices from bean buyers. These buyers profit as middlemen doing most of the buying for major coffee companies.

One coffee company that offers fair trade products is Salt Spring Island Coffee. All the beans ever bought, roasted, and ground by this small company are grown on certified organic farming cooperatives with shade-grown coffee bushes. In 2007, Salt Spring Island Coffee became one of the first carbon-neutral coffee companies in the world. It's coming closer all the time to its goal of zero waste.

CHOCOLATE

Many chocolate bars are inexpensive treats, sold for a dollar or two in stores throughout Western nations. But some chocolate bars cost two

INTERNATIONAL SYMBOLS

There are several symbols used by international associations to certify that a product is made and marketed according to fair trade standards, including FAIRTRADE Mark and Transfair USA. These associations try to make their symbols as recognizable and reliable as the recycling symbol. They are learning from the experiences of the organic food certification process. Each fair trade association awards its symbols to products that meet its standards and provide a good example for other businesses.

or three times as much. The labels of these bars carry registered symbols to show that this chocolate is a certified organic and fair trade product. Can one chocolate bar really be worth three times as much as another one? Can a symbol printed on the wrapper really help you know that? The answer is yes.

Compare the Hershey's bar, made by an American company, with the Noir, made by Schocolade Elysia, a German company. Both companies are more than a hundred years old. The Hershey's bar weighs 1.5 ounces (43 grams), of which 11 percent is cocoa. The Noir weighs 3.5 ounces (100 g), of which 70 percent is cocoa. The Hershey's bar is made by a company that is trying to distance itself from the cheap labor of more than 240,000 children on African plantations. As for the Noir, it carries a fair trade symbol. Taste tests show that for many people, one-third or two-thirds of an ounce (10 or 20 g) of a bar containing 70 percent or more cocoa is more satisfying than

This young worker harvests cacao pods on a cacao plantation in the Ivory Coast. A third of that country's cocoa is exported to the United States for chocolate.

an entire common candy bar. And it has fewer calories. It's true that a 3.5-ounce (100 g) fair trade chocolate bar is often sold for three times the price of a common candy bar. But it also has at least five servings. Look at the quality of a product, not just its price.

Chocolate is made by adding sugar, and sometimes milk products, to cocoa. Much cheaper chocolate candy contains wax and preservatives, too. Cocoa powder and cocoa butter are made from cacao beans, which are the seeds of the *Theobroma cacao* plant. Just because it's called a bean doesn't mean it grows in a pod on a small green vine. Cacao beans are seeds that are inside a football-shaped fruit that grows on a tree pruned to be short. Small insects pollinate the flowers.

Consumers should also be aware of the conditions under which many farmers that sell cacao beans work. It may be hard for U.S. farmers to realize, but until recently, Central American farmers could sell their cacao beans only to a dealer. These dealers would not release the full payment for the beans until the chocolate companies paid their bills in full, often months later. The price for cacao beans fluctuates wildly. The farmers often cannot read or do arithmetic well enough to tell if they have received the full amount that they are owed. The situation in the Ivory Coast in Africa is even worse. There, the cheapest prices are paid for cacao beans harvested by child laborers. They work in fields sprayed with agricultural chemicals. The International Labor Organization stated at the United Nations' 2008 Global Initiative to Fight Human Trafficking (GIFT) that at least twelve thousand of the child cacao workers surveyed in the Ivory Coast were not working with their families but were slaves trafficked from Mali.

A chocolate company that sets the bar high for fair trade goods is Green & Black's Organic Chocolate, based in London, England. The company began production in 1991 when Craig Sams, founder of the Whole Earth organic food company, and his wife, Josephine Fairley, tasted a sample bar of organic 70 percent chocolate. Three years later, their new Maya Gold bar was released. A holiday trip let them see how cacao farmers were vulnerable to price swings in the market. Candy companies drive down the price of beans. Dealers withhold payments. Green & Black's decided to bring its ordinary business standards to an industry that often exploits cacao farmers. The company paid a fair and consistent price for cacao beans. It paid in full when the beans were bought, instead of making partial payments months later. Green & Black's Maya Gold bar was the first product in the United Kingdom to be awarded the FAIRTRADE Mark, in 1994.

The example of fair trade products has influenced mainstream companies. The U.S. chocolate industry is beginning to change. "A mutual benefit is a shared benefit; a shared benefit will endure," says the Web site for Mars Incorporated, a family-owned business.

MAYA GOLD

BITTERSWEET
DARK CHOCOLATE WITH
ORANGE AND SPICES
NET WT. 3.5oz (100g)

FAIR TRADE

Read labels to see if products, such as this Maya Gold organic chocolate bar, are fair trade. For most foods and goods, a fair share of the profits will go to the producer only if there is a fair trade label.

"Mutuality describes the standard to which everyone at Mars aspires in all our business relationships."

CLOTHES

Clothes are essential on a mid-winter day in Canada's Northwest Territories or on a mid-summer day in Phoenix, Arizona. But most of the time, clothes are luxury items that people choose to wear. Clothes are usually not essential to keep people alive. In every country around the world, people choose to wear clothing for modesty and decoration.

It's fun to find the clothes you want at a price you can afford. If you've ever taken a sewing class, you know how hard it is to make clothing well and affordably. So, why do some clothes cost so much less in a store than if you bought fabric and made your own? The clothes cost less because they are cheaply made. The fabric is not the high quality found in fabric stores in Western nations. The work to sew the clothes was done without paying a living wage.

Buying cheaply made clothing manufactured overseas means you're paying for people in foreign countries to do a job that you wouldn't or couldn't do. These people often work for less money than what would be considered enough to live on. They might work for ten or more hours each day in sweatshop conditions that you wouldn't tolerate. The workers who make cheap clothing don't have the protections you enjoy from labor laws, fire safety regulations, and public health measures. Worksite doors are often locked, which traps them inside if there's a fire. Many of the workers are women or children and are usually paid less than men. They are at risk of being beaten by their bosses to work harder for longer hours.

Some stores in Western nations sell clothes only from factories that pay a living wage. Other stores and factories sponsor community development programs. The next time you're buying a pair of overalls to wear during a summer job, do some research. You could buy

Adam Neiman founded Bienestar International, a manufacturer of union-made clothing and footwear called No Sweat. No Sweat is a pioneer in fair trade fashion; it provides consumers with competitively priced products and provides workers with a living wage.

overalls that include a union label showing that the workers formed a union for a fair contract and that the garment will last through dozens of machine washings. When your summer job is over, the overalls could be given to charity. Or, you could buy cheap pants that can tear after you've worn them only a month and which might have been made by a teenage girl working next to her mother and little brother.

APPLYING WHAT YOU KNOW

Each of these three kinds of products—chocolate, coffee, and clothes—has information available that you can track down. You can know what you are using and where the money you spend is going. Read labels. Ask questions when you go into a business. Do Internet searches among company Web sites. It only takes a little looking for you to find out where the materials come from in a product that you use. It may take more searching to find out who profits when you buy and use a product. Become familiar with fair trade products. Then, use the experience to help your family make decisions about essential things like food staples, shelter, energy usage, and transportation.

Choose your products wisely. Do buy local fruit in season, or buy apples picked by migrant workers in Washington State's Okanogan Valley. Do not buy fruits that come from fields sprayed with agricultural chemicals or that were picked by underpaid workers. Research alternatives and make informed decisions. A privately owned nuclear power plant using uranium mined by exploited workers makes a lot of electricity. So does a dam that floods traditional Innu lands in northern Quebec to sell electricity to New York City. And so does a coal-fired plant fueled by strip mining. What about the purchases that you have made? Do you own a bicycle? Maybe you are riding a fixed-up, second-hand bicycle built to last. Or is your bike an inexpensive model built to wear out in a year? There is no one right answer for any of these decisions. There are plenty of reasons for any of the answers that you may choose.

Everything people eat was grown and picked by someone. Buying products with fair trade labels will earn the workers a fair share of the profits made.

Even young people can become informed. Prepare yourself for making decisions in all of these areas. When you begin a career or start a business of your own, apply what you've learned about fair trade business practices. Fair trade is about treating everyone who works with respect. It's about giving other people the same fair deal that you would like to have in your own work and community.

barter Trade by exchanging goods or services, instead of money.

brazing A joining process that is used in manufacturing and that is hotter than soldering and cooler than welding.

carbon-neutral Not releasing a net increase of carbon dioxide into the air by using cleaner methods or by planting trees to use up the carbon dioxide, which is believed to cause global climate change.

certified organic Describing products that have been tested and meet the standards of international organic organizations.

civil disobedience Public protest that is lawful and not violent.

colonialism The economic and governmental dominance of one or more industrialized nations over other nations that are usually less industrialized.

commerce Trade by selling goods or services for money.

community development Programs to develop the services that support a community, such as infrastructure, small businesses, and cultural activities.

consumer A person who buys and uses a product, and for whose attention most advertising is intended.

cooperatives Groups of people that share ownership of a company and the marketing of its products.

ecology The study of the natural world; the interaction of plants and animals in their local environments.

environmentally sustainable Describing methods of using natural resources that minimize pollution and maintain the ecology of an area, including recycling programs and responsible management of resources.

FAIRTRADE Mark A symbol of fair trade products certified by the Fairtrade Federation in England; one of many similar symbols by fair trade organizations.

globalization The process of increasing connections among the world's markets and businesses, made faster because of the technology for travel and communication.

hydrocarbon A chemical made from petroleum, or crude oil, containing carbon and hydrogen.

infrastructure The system of buildings, transportation systems, water and power systems, services, and education that supports a nation.

living wage Sufficient income to provide the necessities and comforts that are important to a satisfactory standard of living.

petrochemical A chemical made from petroleum, or crude oil.

recumbent Lying down.

sustainable development Use of a resource in ways that support the local economy and maintain the local environment.

toxic Poisonous or harmful to one's health.

vulnerable Able to be harmed.

FOR MORE INFORMATION

Council on International and Public Affairs (CIPA)
P.O. Box 337 (52 Grand Street)
Croton on Hudson, NY 10520
(800) 316-2739
Web site: http://www.cipa-apex.org
The CIPA is a nonprofit research, education, and publishing group that
analyzes significant economic, social, and political issues in the
United States and around the world.

Fair Labor Association USA (FLA)
1707 L Street NW, Suite 200
Washington, DC 20036
(202) 898-1000
Web site: http://www.fairlabor.org
The FLA is a nonprofit organization dedicated to building innovative
and sustainable solutions to abusive labor conditions.

Fair Trade Federation
3025 Fourth Street NE, Suite 107
Washington, DC 20017-1102
(202) 636-3547
Web site: http://www.fairtradefederation.org
This is an association of Canadian and American fair trade wholesalers,
importers, and retailers.

Fairtrade Labeling Organizations International
Bonner Talweg 177
53120 Bonn
Germany

Web site: http://www.fairtrade.net
This international association of trade organizations provides labeling
    initiatives and networks.

Global Exchange
2017 Mission Street, 2nd Floor
San Francisco, CA 94110
(415) 255-7296
Web site: http://www.globalexchange.org
Global Exchange is an education and action resource center that for
    twenty years has worked for international human rights and social,
    environmental, and economic justice.

Green America
Co-op America Foundation
1612 K Street NW, Suite 600
Washington DC 20006
(800) 584-7336
Web site: http://www.coopamerica.org
Co-op America's Green Business Network is the largest network
    of socially and environmentally responsible businesses
    in America.

International Federation for Alternative Trade (IFAT)
Prijssestraat 24
4104CR Culemborg
The Netherlands
Web site: http://www.ifat.org

The IFAT, also known as the International Fair Trade Association, is the global network of fair trade organizations, with regional centers in Africa, Asia, and Latin America.

International Resources for Fairer Trade (IRFT)
Sona Udyog, Unit No. 7
Parsi Panchayat Road, Andheri (E)
Mumbai—400 069 (Maharasta)
India
Web site: http://www.irft.org/aboutus.html
The IRFT has worked since 1995 to promote business development and monitor socially responsible behavior among mainstream businesses.

Oxfam America
226 Causeway Street, 5th floor
Boston, MA 02114
(800) 776-9326
Web site: http://www.oxfamamerica.org

Oxfam Canada
National Office
250 City Centre Avenue, Suite 400
Ottawa, ON K1R 6K7
Canada
(613) 237-5236
Web site: http://www.oxfam.ca
Oxfam works worldwide to prevent hunger, poverty, and social injustice.

TreePeople
12601 Mulholland Drive
Beverly Hills, CA 90210
(818) 753-4600
Web site: http://www.treepeople.org
TreePeople is a nonprofit organization that offers sustainable solutions
    to help heal urban areas with tree-planting programs.

YouthNoise
1255 Post Street, Suite 1120
San Francisco, CA 94109
(415) 346-4433
Web site: http://www.youthnoise.com
YouthNoise is a nonprofit organization that provides a social networking
    site for young people interested in human rights and social causes.

WEB SITES

Due to the changing nature of Internet links, Rosen Publishing has developed an online list of Web sites related to the subject of this book. This site is updated regularly. Please use this link to access the list:

http://www.rosenlinks.com/gre/fair

FOR FURTHER READING

Cooper, Adrian. *Fair Trade? A Look at the Way the World Is Today*. Mankato, MN: Stargazer Books, 2006.

Decarlo, Jacqueline. *Fair Trade: A Beginner's Guide*. London, England: National Book Network, 2007.

Godin, Seth. *Tribes: We Need You to Lead Us*. New York, NY: Portfolio Hardcover, 2008.

Guillain, Adam, and Elke Steiner. *Bella's Chocolate Surprise*. Chicago, IL: Milet Publishing, 2008.

Henderson, Hazel. *Fair Trade, Ethical Trade* (Ethical Markets Television series). Princeton, NJ: Films for the Humanities & Sciences, 2007.

Leonard, Anne. *The Story of Stuff*. Washington, DC: Free Range Studios, Tides Foundation & Funders Workgroup for Sustainable Production and Consumption, 2008.

Raynolds, Laura. *Fair Trade: The Challenges of Transforming Globalization*. New York, NY: Policy Library, 2007.

Steger, Manfred B. *Globalization: A Very Short Introduction*. Rev. ed. New York, NY: Oxford University Press, 2009.

Vergara, Diane Abad. *Zapizapu Crosses the Sea: A Story About Being Fair*. Victoria, Canada: Trafford Publishing, 2008.

BIBLIOGRAPHY

Armenio, Maribeth. "The Bittersweet in the Sweet." *Immaculata High School Child Slave Labor Newsletter*, December 2006. Retrieved October 24, 2008 (http://ihscslnews.org/view_article.php?id=172).

Ballinger, Jeffrey. "The New Free-Trade Heel: Nike's Profits Jump on the Backs of the Asian Worker." *Harper's*, August 1992, pp. 46–47. Retrieved October 24, 2008 (http://harpers.org/archive/1992/08/0000971).

Broad, Robin. *Global Backlash: Citizen Initiatives for a Just World Economy*. Lanham, MD: Rowman & Littlefield, 2002.

Cherry, Tamara. "Global Forum Targets Horrors of Human Trafficking." *Toronto Sun*, February 14, 2008. Retrieved October 24, 2008 (http://cnews.canoe.ca/CNEWS/World/2008/02/14/4846415-sun.html).

Chouhan, T. R. *Bhopal: The Inside Story—Carbide Workers Speak Out on the World's Worst Industrial Disaster*. New York, NY: The Apex Press, 2004.

Compa, Lance A., and Stephen F. Diamond. *Human Rights, Labor Rights, and International Trade*. Pittsburgh, PA: University of Pennsylvania Press, 2003.

Elliott, Kimberly Ann, and Richard Barry Freeman. *Can Labor Standards Improve Under Globalization?* Washington, DC: Peterson Institute, 2003.

Ellis, Karl. "History Not Repeating." TasmanianTimes.com, May 19, 2008. Retrieved September 4, 2008 (http://tasmaniantimes.com/index.php?/weblog/article/history-not-repeating).

Fridell, Gavin. *Fair Trade Coffee: The Prospects and Pitfalls of Market-Driven Social Justice*. Toronto, Canada: University of Toronto Press, 2007.

GreenLiving.com. "Principles." Retrieved October 2, 2008 (http://www.green-living.com/index.asp?PageAction=Custom&ID=10).

Haft, Jeremy. *All the Tea in China: How to Buy, Sell, and Make Money on the Mainland*. New York, NY: Portfolio Hardcover, 2008.

Katz, Donald. *Just Do It: The Nike Spirit in the Corporate World*. Holbrook, MA: Adams Media, 1994.

Linton, Sara. "The New Air Jordan Is Redesigned for Your Inner Environmentalist." *Ecorazzi: The Latest in Green Gossip*, January 10, 2008. Retrieved October 2, 2008 (http://www.ecorazzi.com/2008/01/10/the-new-air-jordan-is-redesigned-for-your-inner-enviromentalist).

Litvinoff, Miles, and John Madeley. *50 Reasons to Buy Fair Trade*. London, England: Pluto Press, 2007.

Loisel, Laurle. "For Fair Trade, This Kid's on the Ball." *Daily Hampshire Gazette*, May 22, 2008. Retrieved October 22, 2008 (http://www.gazettenet.com/story/184120?CSAuthResp=%3Asession%3ACSUserId%7CCSGroupId%3Asuccess%3AiaII8fM4EuZY0jtgJjbrLg%3D%3D&CSUserId=20597&CSGroupId=7).

Mars Consumer Care Principles. "Mutuality." Retrieved October 2, 2008 (http://www.masterfoodsconsumercare.co.uk/pple_mutuality.asp).

Morgan, Simon. "Film, Pop Stars Headline UN Anti-Human Trafficking Campaign." *Daily News Egypt*, February 13, 2008. Retrieved October 24, 2008 (http://www.dailystaregypt.com/article.aspx?ArticleID=11860).

Nichols, Alex, and Charlotte Opal. *Fair Trade: Market-Driven Ethical Consumption*. London, England: Sage, 2005.

Olson, Geoff. "Clayoquot Was Defining Protest of Our Time: Biosphere Reserve Status Gives No Protection." *Common Ground*, August 2003, p. 27.

Owusu, K. "Cocoa Revealed: The Industry." *The K Experience*, March 24, 2008. Retrieved September 6, 2008 (http://thekexperience.okeiweb.com/present/here-and-now/cocoa-revealed-the-industry.html).

Oxfam International. "Trade Rigged Rules." Retrieved September 2, 2008 (http://www.oxfam.org/en/campaigns/trade).

Ransom, David. *No-Nonsense Guide to Fair Trade*. Oxford, England: New Internationalist Publications, Ltd., 2006.

Read, Richard. "Nike's Focus on Keeping Costs Low Causes Poor Working Conditions, Critics Say." *Oregonian*, August 5, 2008. Retrieved October 25, 2008 (http://www.oregonlive.com/business/oregonian/index.ssf?/base/news/121790850350380.xml&coll=7).

Shaw, Randy. *Reclaiming America: Nike, Clean Air, and the New National Activism*. Berkeley, CA: University of California Press, 1999. Retrieved October 25, 2008 (http://www.ucpress.edu/books/pages/8392/8392.ch01.php).

Skelton, Chad. "Old-Growth Logging Plan Sparks War-in-Woods Threat." *Vancouver Sun*, July 23, 2008. Retrieved September 2, 2008 (http://www.canada.com/vancouversun/news/story.html?id=0448c5f7-10f5-4d72-8634-0577065f7712).

Stiglitz, Joseph E., and Andrew Charlton. *Fair Trade for All: How Trade Can Promote Development*. Rev. ed. Oxford, England: Oxford University Press, 2007.

Swift, Richard. "The Cocoa Chain." *New Internationalist*, Issue 304, August 1998, p. 5.

Trudeau, Garry. "Doonesbury Nike Comic Strips." *Doonesbury*, May 1997. Retrieved October 24, 2008 (http://doonesbury.com and http://www.geocities.com/athens/acropolis/5232/comicmay97.htm).

Underwood, Kirsten. "Kona Donates AfricaBikes to Africa." Treehugger.com, September 11, 2008. Retrieved September 11, 2008 (http://www.treehugger.com/files/2008/09/kona-donates-africabikes-to-africa.php).

West Corporation. "A World of Opportunity." 2006. Retrieved October 2, 2008 (http://www.westemployment.com/aboutwest.asp).

INDEX

ABOUT THE AUTHOR

Paula Johanson has worked as a writer and teacher for more than twenty years, writing and editing nonfiction books on science, health, and literature. She operated an organic method market garden for fifteen years, selling produce and sheep's wool at farmer's markets. At two or more conferences each year, Johanson leads panel discussions on practical science and how it applies to home life and creative work. An accredited teacher, she has written and edited educational materials for the Alberta Distance Learning Centre in Canada.

PHOTO CREDITS

Cover, p. 1 © www.istockphoto.com/Anja Hild; pp. 7, 15, 47 © AP Images; p. 8 Per-Anders Pettersson/Getty Images; p. 10 © www.istockphoto.com/ranplett; p. 10 (inset) © www.istockphoto.com/Jayson Punwani; p. 12 AFP/Getty Images; p. 20 © Andrew Fox/Corbis; p. 23 © Andy Aitchison/Corbis; p. 24 © Keith I. Cozzens/Kona Bicycle Company; p. 27 © Bruno Fert/Corbis; p. 30 Alan Dejecacion/Getty Images; p. 35 Moe Doiron/KRT Photos/Newscom.com; p. 36 Scott Barbour/Getty Images; p. 40 © Paul Souders/Corbis; p. 43 Issouf Sanogo/AFP/Getty Images; p. 43 (inset) © www.istockphoto.com/ALEAIMAGE; p. 49 dpa/Newscom.com.

Designer: Nicole Russo; Editor: Kathy Kuhtz Campbell;
Photo Researcher: Amy Feinberg